Sparkles

A magical story of transformation

Written by
Michal Y. Noah, Ph.D.

Illustrated by
Favreau

Text and Illustrations Copyright © 2016 by Michal Y. Noah

All rights reserved. No part of this publication may be reproduced, distributed, or transmitted in any form or by any means, including photocopying, recording, or other electronic or mechanical methods, without the prior written permission of the publisher, except in the case of brief quotations embodied in critical reviews and cer‹tain other noncommercial uses permitted by copyright law. For permission requests, write to the publisher, addressed "Attention: Permissions Coordinator," at the address below.

A Magical World in You, Inc.
Huntingdon Valley, PA 19006
www.michalynoah.com

Hardcover ISBN 978-0-9967757-1-7
Paperback ISBN 978-0-9908394-9-1

Library of Congress Control Number: 2016903828

This is a work of fiction. Names, characters, businesses, places, events and incidents are either the products of the author's imagination or used in a fictitious manner. Any resemblance to actual persons, living or dead, or actual events is purely coincidental.

Ordering Information:

Quantity sales. Special discounts are available on quantity purchases by corporations, associations, and others. For details, contact the publisher at the address above.

Printed in the United States of America.

AUTHOR'S NOTE

I've always felt that we are born with unique gifts and talents and that there is more in us than what we allow to emerge. There is such greatness within ourselves that if we were to let it surface and bloom, it would enrich the world to unimaginable levels.

At times, we are unknowingly harsh on ourselves; instead of being comfortable with our greatness, we tone it down and turn down our own inner light, not permitting full expression of the magical beings we really are.

I've written my fourth book, *Sparkles,* especially for children so that they look within themselves and identify, acknowledge, embrace, and share their unique gifts with the world.

As parents, family members, and teachers, we should encourage children to be aware that they are truly magical and that it's okay to be themselves and shine their unique, brilliant light on the world. We all have this inner knowledge that we are capable of being and doing much more; it is good to nurture this potential and reinforce this belief in children so that they grow up with this self-awareness.

With much love and joy,

Michal Noah

"Sparkles is my name," she said,
"And this story is about me.
If you listen closely to my tale,
It's quite magical, you'll agree."

"You now see me as a butterfly
That's so happy, joyful, and free.
But I wasn't always like this.
I looked very different, you see."

Inside a teensy-weensy egg,
That's where her life began.
Afraid she'd stay locked up inside
Escape was Sparkles' plan.

"Let me out! Please, let me out.
It's too cramped here. It's too tight.
Get me out of this gloomy place.
I want to see the beautiful light."

"Hello, is there someone out there?
Hey, can anyone hear me at all?
Please, oh, please, help me come out.
Won't someone listen to my call?"

"I want to get out and explore
I know there's more that I can be.
I'm sure I was born for greater things,
There must be more than I can see."

Sparkles tried to move and kick around.
She could feel she was on her way.
With just a little bit more effort,
She'd soon see the light of the day.

It was time to step out from there,
There was much to see and lots to do.
She pushed to the left, then to the right,
And finally broke through!

"Magical world, how beautiful you are!
And here I am, outside at last.
All that I want to do for now
Is play and eat and grow real fast."

"For now, I'll just focus on my meals.
I can't seem to stop eating, you see.
I'm sure there's more to life than this,
Something better is lined up for me."

Sparkles sat on a giant green leaf
And munched on it for so long.
Before she knew it, she became
Big and large and really strong.

As she kept nibbling on the leaves,
Something inside her seemed to say,
"That's not all there is to living.
There's more you can become every day."

It was a soft whisper that she heard,
A gentle voice that seemed to say,
"There's more to life than this.
A caterpillar you're not going to stay."

Sparkles wondered what life was like up above.
She wished she, too, could go up so high.
Like the birdies and the bees around her,
How she wished that she too could fly.

"I won't spend all my life like this,
There must be more for me to see.
I can't be crawling on the ground all day.
I know there's more that I can be."

She couldn't ignore her inner voice,
It forced her to ponder and think.
Sparkles was tired and wanted to sleep.
In a bed of soft leaves, she wished to sink.

"That voice is right, I'm pretty sure,
But I need time to think this through.
Tomorrow is another new day.
I'll take a long nap. That's what I'll do."

"I'll build myself a sleeping bag,
In which I can snuggle so deep.
All I'll do is spin one and zip it up.
I'll close my eyes and go to sleep."

Sparkles started to weave her little bag,
Seeming to know exactly what to do;
She spun herself a cozy chrysalis
In which she'd sleep for a week or two.

She kept wondering who she really was
And what she could possibly be.
She got the feeling there was more to her,
Much more than what she now could see.

Sparkles closed her eyes and thought hard
About what that voice told her so sweetly.
She just knew it; she could feel it.
Yes, there was more in her that she could be.

Sparkles dreamt that she was flying.
She had wings that kissed the sun.
She felt so happy and so free.
Flying felt like so much fun.

After many days of dreaming,
Once again, she heard the same whisper.
"It's time to wake up and fly, little one.
C'mon, tear open your bag's zipper."

As she cast off her chrysalis
And was out of it at last,
Sparkles couldn't wait a moment more,
She wanted to see the world real fast.

She turned her head from side to side.
She stretched to her left and then to her right.
What a pretty pair of sparkly wings!
They are such a lovely sight!

"Oh, this is so difficult to believe!
Oh, my! Could that really be me?
Such magnificent sparkling wings,
They're too pretty to be mine, you see."

"I've always dreamt of such pretty wings,
But I'm scared to open them and fly.
They're prettier than the prettiest ones.
Yet my inner voice tells me I must try."

"Sparkles is your name, my dear.
Remember, there is magic in you.
You can be what you want to be
And do what you want to do."

"I have to realize my potential.
I must not forget that.
I should be the best I can be
And do best what I'm good at."

"I am unique, I am special,
I am just outstanding!
Now it's time to take-off!
I can figure out the landing."

Sparkles spread her sparkly wings
And took off and flew up so high.
Knowing they'd never let her down,
She was off on her way to the sky.

"Yes, I was right after all, you see.
I knew that this could only be true.
There certainly is magic within me.
Look at what I now can do!"

"Each one of us is special.
Through my story, you now know
There is magic within you, too.
Just let your inner light glow."

Other Books by Michal Noah, Ph.D.

A-Z: The Universe in Me

The Magic Tree

I'll See You in My Dreams

www.ingramcontent.com/pod-product-compliance
Lightning Source LLC
Chambersburg PA
CBHW061932290426
44113CB00024B/2882